Write
and
Grow Rich

Deondrica Cantrice

Way, Inc
Prosper, TX

Way, Inc
ISBN: 979-8-8689-3135-2

PRINTED IN THE UNITED STATES OF AMERICA

Dedication

This book is dedicated to all authors and aspiring writers who possess the discipline to pen a book and the courage to share their gift with the world. I honor you and your passion for the craft.
~Deondriea Cantrice

Table of Contents

Foreword

Rich: /riCH/ *adjective having a great deal of money or assets; wealthy.*

When most people hear the word "rich", they think of gold-paved streets, hundred-dollar bills that hang freely from pockets and the luxurious life that wealth affords you. While some people envision their favorite celebrity as being "rich," others would raise an eyebrow to the correlation. You see, being rich goes beyond having money. As a writer with either dreams to be published or dreams of watching your published book prosper, we all desire to make money from our passion. That's a given. However, being rich and having money are not always one-in-the same.

If someone could put a price on the passions in your heart, one of which is probably writing or else you wouldn't be reading this book, do you think there's a dollar amount that could equate to it? For most people the answer is no. The passions, gifts, desires and goals in your heart and soul cannot be bought, sold or Groupon'd to the highest bidder.

The very meaning of your passions, gifts and goals is, in all actuality, your life's purpose. While most people search their entire lives for their life's purpose, with bank accounts filled with money, there are others who are blessed to have found theirs with a good, but not Bill Gates, bank account. So who's to say who is "richer"?

As a writer, you are one of the most feared dreamers alive. People can't understand how or why you do what you do with such certainty in an industry of such uncertainty. If you're a true dreamer, that last statement made you smile; you know your purpose and are ready for the ride. But, don't underestimate the obstacles that will be in your path as a dreamer who dreams of writing. Be prepared for them, instead. Welcome them, embrace them, because you don't truly grasp the wealth of your passion until it has been tested, tried and laughed at. That's why it's so important to write not solely for the monetary gain, but for the fulfillment of your life's purpose/plan. Your God-given talent will never leave you. It's in for the long-haul.

Most people have no idea what their gift from God is. If you're lucky, you do. If you're blessed and in-tune with your gift, you'll be able to feed your life's purpose while also making money along the way. But understand this, discovering your gift is its own priceless pot of gold. Discovering your gift is one thing, using it is another. I once heard that the richest place on earth is the graveyard because there are so many never-before-used talents there. Don't be one of those people who know their gift, but fail to use it. Find your undeniable, priceless wealth in the satisfaction of your gift, the one God Himself gave you, by putting it to use.

There are many levels of being rich as an author, but I want to make sure we touch on the most important:

richness in self. Yes, you can end up on every Best-Selling list known to man, or have hundreds of interviews promoting your work. You may even be blessed to have your book of work turned into a movie: It is possible. The steps are simple: know your gift, appreciate your gift, use your gift, work for your gift and watch your gift work for you.

Being rich is something that people have been chasing forever and I doubt it will ever stop. Still, you can have a one-up on the competition when you realize that your God-given talent, your desire to do what you know you were put on earth to do, has already placed you in the "richer than most" category. You can only reach higher levels of success, with monetary and non-monetary gain from there. Be open to the many levels of success that come from being a writer.

How you view things will ultimately determine how you view your own success. Writing goes beyond sitting at a keyboard and writing anything that comes to mind. It takes structure, commitment, dedication and sometimes sacrifices. Likewise, being wealthy goes beyond just having money in the bank and name brand clothes on your back. Being wealthy takes structure, commitment, dedication and sometimes, sacrifices. See the correlation? Stay consistent with both in order to attain (and keep them).

You will be your greatest critic, fan and think-tank. Listen to yourself and watch how you (and your God-given gift) take you and others to heights unknown! In **Write and Grow Rich**, National Best Selling Author, Deondriea

Cantrice will show you how to take those talents and use those gifts to become rich on levels you never dreamed possible.

Enjoy the journey,

Elissa Gabrielle
President & CEO, Peace In The Storm Publishing USA
TODAY recommended Author

Acknowledgements

To Kadena Tate, my friend and business coach. You are absolutely amazing! Thank you for showing me how all the pieces fit together.

Special thanks to Otis Spears. I sincerely appreciate all of your hard work and creative talent that you have invested in me. Without you it would be difficult for me to do what I do. Thank you.

Introduction

Everyone has a voice and a story to tell. The key is having the ability to tell a story that compels people to want to read it, tell others about it, and continue to buy your book!

Is having something to write about and knowing how to write enough to become a successful author? The answer is NO! From the onset of early education throughout continuing education, there are hundreds of thousands of courses and classes that teach us how to write. But no one teaches us how to be an author and more importantly how to be a successful author.

There are classes, seminars, webinars, blogs articles, and every other form of medium that comes to mind that offers a plan on how to successfully market your book. What makes **Write and Grow Rich** unique? As a successful writer, I understand that most people don't have the time or the interest to sift through mountains of material that reads like stereo instructions and is more complicated than the Holy Grail. Nor, would it be wise to spend endless amounts of money to purchase additional resources only to discover information that is embarrassingly simple and is backed with useless information that doesn't assist you in achieving your specific goals.

I have decided to condense my experience, knowledge, and resources as an author and marketing professional into an easy to read, snapshot of what you can do as an author to successfully market yourself and your book.

Yes, I offer courses to give you a more granular look into how to establish your brand as an author and how to apply the tools necessary to become a successful author. But this book is enough to get you started down the right path, or change your direction towards your goal of being a successful author!

How do you know which marketing strategy is best for you? I will be honest with you. There is not a single "right" answer. There is not a one size fits all solution that is applicable in the literary world. Where you are in your literary career, your publishing category and genre, your finances and a variety of other factors will determine which marketing plan will lead you towards your literary objectives. The key is to have a plan and be ready to implement it.

In this book, you will be introduced to several theories and options to help you develop a marketing strategy for your literary works. Some of the marketing options you will find useful, while other strategies may not be applicable to your goals. What's important is that you know what works for you, your resources and your book.

Write and Grow Rich is a roadmap, not a blueprint. The benefit of a roadmap is, it guides you to a specific destination from wherever you are. Whereas, a blueprint is designed to be a step by step guide from ground level, with prearranged steps, to create a predetermined outcome with no variations.

The literary world has become oversaturated with books about everything, from everyone. The passion to write has been diminished by the desire to hustle and the ease of self-publishing. There is nothing wrong with getting paid for your works, but know your craft and be willing to do the work. Due to the oversaturation, it is increasingly harder to be noticed, so you have to be willing to do what others may not be.

I encourage you to grab a pencil, highlighter or whatever it will take to make this book work for you. Think of this book as a workbook and reference guide rather than reading material. ***Write and Grow Rich's*** interactive format will challenge you to think, be creative, and analyze your plan of action towards becoming a successful writer.

Everyone assumes that their big break is waiting for them, which is partly true. Your big break as a successful author is waiting for you, but discovering where the big break lies is the challenge. If you are simply searching for overnight success, this book is not for you! As you *grow*, think of it this way, you are planted, with deep roots, blooming, and endless growth opportunities. Being a rising star offers more longevity than a shooting star. By growing, you will attract all the success that you desire.

You have already made the most important step by picking up this book. There will be action items for you at the end of each chapter and pages for notes to help nudge you along by stirring your creative juices. Strategic implementation will be what moves you from being a person that wrote a book to being a successful author. Now is a great time to…

Write and Grow Rich!

You Wrote a Book, Now What?

Congratulations! You had the patience, focus, and ambition to pen a book. Now what do you do with it? Just when you thought you completed a monumental task, the real work begins. Whether you are already published or looking to be published, there is still a lot of work to be done. You have successfully written and/or published a book, now it's time to make that book a success.

In **Write and Grow Rich**, I will provide the necessary material for you to build the foundation of what to do once you are ready to publish, if you are newly published, or if you are facing the challenge of how to move your book from the shelf into the hands of readers.

In the literary world today, there are *traditional, vanity* and *independent publishers.* And, of course you have the option to *self-publish.* The benefit of having several publishing options is that everyone can get published. The problem with having so many publishing options is that everyone can get published!

With such a variety of publishing options available, as an author, you are affected by trends just like any other industry. These trends include but are not limited to pricing, shelf space and of course reader expectations. More importantly, there is more competition for visibility, as well as more authors with their hands in the reader's pockets.

Because this book focuses on marketing your works and not publishing, I will not go into a lot of detail about publishing options. However, the publishing option that you choose will affect your marketing efforts.

Most authors dream of a book deal with a traditional publisher and a marketing team that is second to none that will provide them with visibility and opportunities. As I have already stated, each publishing option has both benefits and deficits. A publishing deal doesn't negate your responsibility to market, it just changes how much you will market and promote your book(s) on your own.

Traditional publishers are bombarded with query letters from writers that are looking to be published. Depending on the publisher, it may take up to six months before your works are even reviewed. And, after all that waiting your book may not be accepted. With a traditional publisher you may lose some of your creative control, and you are required to meet several other requirements as outlined in your contract that can include but is not limited to your book title, cover, publication date, and commissions.

The plus side of signing with a traditional publisher is that you will have the prestige of a mainstream publisher backing your work, which means major bookstores are more likely to carry your books without additional efforts by you. Also there may be an option for advances and other perks that vary by publisher.

A vanity publisher is a publishing company that authors pay an upfront fee to have their books published. Publishing with a vanity publisher gives you several of the same benefits offered by traditional publishers like issuing an ISBN, national distribution, and accounting efforts. Sometimes, vanity presses are not selective with what or who they publish. In fact, some vanity presses don't even take the time to read the manuscript prior to publication.

A vanity publisher is a great option for aspiring authors that want to test the literary waters because it will allow you to maintain more creative control of your works, and still have benefits like world-wide distribution and other benefits of having a publisher. However, in some arenas, vanity publishers are not recognized with the same prestige of a traditional publisher. For example, it's harder to get shelf space with a vanity publisher.

Vanity publishers offer more independence and flexibility than the traditional publishers, but the profit margin for the author is sometimes lower and the quality of the book is sometimes compromised. Although a vanity publisher will offer marketing services at an additional fee, it's still a good idea to have a marketing plan of your own. Some authors use a vanity publisher to print limited copies of the book to fulfill a short term need or desire and to build a fan base before transitioning into other publishing options.

Independent publishers, fall somewhere between a vanity and a traditional publisher. The beauty of an independent publisher is they sometimes limit the number of authors they publish. In some cases they chose a particular genre that they publish. Being selective allows the publisher to build better relationships with their authors.

Although most independent publishers are very selective about the books and authors that they publish, they allow their authors to exercise more creative control than traditional publishers. And, because independent publishers are usually small, they are sometimes willing to invest more into the success of your book because they have more at stake.

When people think of self-publishing, most people automatically assume that this option will equate to greater financial success. The thought is *if I have less people lobbying for their share of the dollars that I earn, it will result in a greater net income for me*. That is not always the case and here is why. Every single thing you do is your responsibility, and those responsibilities sometimes carry healthy price tags, i.e. printing, distribution, promotions, and many other administrative tasks which add up very quickly when you haven't even sold your first book.

There are two ways to self-publish. One option is to set up a publishing company, which includes an EIN (employer identification number), registering with the Secretary of State, and setting up corporate accounts. This particular option is good because vendors and other companies will take you more seriously. The other option is to simply pen a book, print it and attempt to sell your books out the trunk of your car.

Again, both options have their fair share of ups and downs. How much time are you willing to invest in selling and pitching your book to potential readers? Do you want to spend your resources networking with stores to carry your book? When you choose to go to a printer instead of through a distributor to sell your books on your own, you spend more money than you think.

Just as a quick note to remember, most traditional bookstores will not carry books that don't have an ISBN. And, if your book is not listed with one of the two major book distributors some bookstores and libraries will also opt against carrying your book. If your book doesn't have an ISBN, you will limit your sales and distribution opportunities.

Of course there are a few authors who have been very successful by selling their books out of the trunk of their car. But they were willing to be present, consistent and invest their time. You have to possess the drive to hustle an extensive amount of hours of the day and knock on as many doors as possible in order to generate the desired results from your book.

Whenever I speak to aspiring authors, I always encourage them to explore all publishing options before choosing one option over another. Each publishing choice presents its fair share of pros and cons, in addition to varied levels of commitment of time and other resources. I cannot recommend which option is better or worse. However, I can advise you to know what your expectations and objectives are not only from your book, but from a publisher as well. I also advise you to be well aware of what a publisher requires of you.

Literary marketing not only takes work, it takes a planned strategy. Everyone has a dream of that big contract with a well-known, traditional publisher. But, the harsh truth is traditional publishers are publishing fewer authors each year. Most traditional publishers even require that you have a solid fan base and steady book sales before they will sign you.

Even with the name of a traditional publisher behind you, there is still work required from you and/or your team to make your book a success. There is still the need for branding, marketing, and the promotion of your book, which will attract the attention of a traditional publisher. So don't get hung up on publishing with a traditional publisher when your focus should be on delivering a good read to the world.

There are a couple of key items that has to be in place first before you can create an effective marketing plan. The title and cover of your book are equally, if not more important than its contents. The cover should catch the reader's eye and the contents have to hold their attention.

The title of your book is the first introduction readers will have to you and/or your book(s). Sometimes the title alone is all a reader sees or hears. The title of your book should be something catchy, clever and creative. You may consider the use of play on words, or something that will be easy for readers to remember. The title of book should intrigue readers to pick up your book, thumb through its pages or investigate the book a little further. Never choose a title that is misleading and avoid titles that disclose the plot, unless your book is non-fiction; in that case you want readers to know exactly what they have in store.

The title of my first book is *Rhythm Can't Keep Time, Sometimes Love Just Ain't Enough*. As a new writer, people were interested in my book for no other reason than the contradictory title. Readers wanted to know exactly what my book was all about. They didn't expect it to be a realistic look about relationships through an erotic lens.

When you think of a title for your book, think of it as if you are naming a child. When naming a child you decide on a name that you like, knowing the child will have to carry it their entire life. You don't name your child something and change it in a year or the first time someone says they don't like it. Parallel the name of your book in that same manner. Be sure the title of your book is something you can be proud of and is everlasting.

To my author friends that write street literature, you may want to be mindful of the use of profanity in the title. Strong profanity on the cover may limit places where your book will be carried and definitely how it's placed in the stores. And, you don't want readers to be embarrassed to read your book while commuting, at the office or in front of mixed company.

Along with the title of your book, the book cover has to speak to potential readers. Think of your cover design as a gift you are giving to the world. Because humans are visual people, your cover may stop someone in their tracks because they are attracted to the cover and develop a genuine interest of the contents inside.

Here are a few questions that you can ask yourself to ensure that your title represents you and your book.

- How does the cover design apply to the book?

- Is it professionally designed?

- What emotion do you want readers to feel when they see your book cover?

- Does the title of my book draw attention?

- Is my book cover professional and appealing?

By now you are probably anxious to get to how to make money selling your book. I had to address the publishing options, title and cover before I could give you tools of the trade. These tools will prove to be useless if your book is less than a quality product. You owe it to readers to deliver a book that is properly edited, professionally formatted and creatively packaged. You have to take pride and believe in the product that you are selling in order for others to see the value in it.

ACTION ITEMS

1. Determine how much time you are willing to invest in advertising and promoting your book?

2. If you haven't already published, research and decide which publishing option is best for you?

3. If you are already published, what support can you expect from your publishing company as it relates to marketing your book?

NOTES

NOTES

NOTES

NOTES

Come Out Wherever You Are!

Let's discuss "Kevin." Only because he is a former client and a dear friend I will use him as an example. Of course Kevin is not his real name, but I have to protect the identity of the guilty. Kevin is a reformed gang member and former drug dealer that decided to draft his story of doom to destiny in order to inspire today's youth.

When I met Kevin several years ago, he was frustrated, ready to throw in the towel and kiss a career as a writer good-bye. He had written a book, self-published it and purchased 5000 copies of his book to sell. Two years later, he had barely sold 500 books. This was extremely hard for someone that took his passion from making fast money to making a difference in the lives of others.

Kevin's book was a children's book that focused on bullying. Because he once was a gang member he was able to offer great content on the importance of staying in school and protecting yourself against bullying.

Before I took him on as a client, I didn't understand why he wasn't more successful and in the midst of his third or fourth print run considering bullying in schools was such a hot topic at the time. He was so frustrated because people told him it was a great book but no one was buying it. Kevin was beginning to think that everyone was lying to him. Were they? No. I thought the book was a great read, with good illustrations.

I began to do my research on Kevin and his book. In less than 5 minutes into his assessment, it was obvious his book wasn't selling like hot cakes. Kevin had plenty of books and bookmarks. And, that's all folks! None of Kevin's branding collateral had his contact information on it, which defeats the purpose of branding.

Kevin self-published without establishing a publishing company through the proper channels, which meant his book was not listed with any book retailers or available online. There was no barcode or any other publisher information to be found on his book. He simply paid someone to format and print his books, nothing more. He was literally selling books out the trunk of his car, which is not a problem if it is strategically done. He did not have a website or a page on any social media sites. I had to ask Kevin,

"How do you expect to become a bestselling author if no one knows that you exist?"

"Everyone who has read the book loves it. Do you think they just didn't want to hurt my feelings?" he asked.

Kevin's response absolutely floored me. It was not a question of his book being good; it was that no one knew about it or where to find it.

"If I love your book, where do I buy another copy? Or where should I send other people to buy a copy of their own?" I asked.

"They can always get copies from me." He responded.

"Ok, where can I find you, if I don't know you personally?" I asked.

Kevin just stared at me with a confused look on his face. If that interaction wasn't a classic case of ineffective communication, I don't know what is. I grabbed a bag out of my office that I take to book signings, took a few items out of the bag and laid them on the table. I asked Kevin what he noticed about my items. He said,

"You have a lot of stuff" and chuckled.

I couldn't help but smile at him as he looked clueless at all the promotional material that I had placed on the table. I pointed out that all my material included where people could find me. Whether it was my books, banners, business cards or giveaways, I had my website, address, and/or my phone number on each of the items. I ensured that people could find me by whatever their preferred method of communication was.

"See Kevin, this is why my books sell. I leave no guess work for the reader. I make sure they don't have to look for me. I am visible."

Kevin's situation was a challenge for me because he self-published without an ISBN or barcode. How could I help him develop an effective marketing campaign when brick and mortar or online book retailers wouldn't carry his book? I used the fact that he was a "hustler" to create him an effective marketing campaign.

The first step that I took in developing his campaign was I created labels for him to affix on the inside of the back cover of his book that included his contact information. With about 4500 books to get rid of this was the best quick fix option that I could come up with.

To be honest, the story that Kevin had to tell was better than the book he was selling. His best option was to market himself as a speaker that has a book rather than as an author. The plan I created for Kevin included a media kit and a target list of people and places to mail it to.

I bet you are wondering why I didn't encourage Kevin to get a website. I didn't go that route because Kevin had spent the bulk of his young adult life in jail. He wasn't tech savvy and he wasn't too eager to embrace it either. And, it would have done more harm than good for him to launch an online marketing campaign because he was unwilling to manage or pay someone to manage an online initiative for him.

Kevin will answer the phone and occasionally will respond to email. But I knew it would be next to impossible for him create, interact and follow up with anyone reaching out to him in cyberspace. I gave him the names of a couple vanity publishing companies that would reprint his book, so he could gain more visibility and have book retailers pick up his book once he had depleted his current inventory of books.

Let me introduce you to Tyrone, another client. Tyrone used one of those online self-publishing companies. Although he had an ISBN and barcode, he still was responsible for his own marketing.

Tyrone established a strong online presence to sell his books. He hired me because his sales had flat-lined and he could not figure out why. I researched Tyrone and discovered he was only promoting his books to people that he knew. The problem with that is he was not connected to many people online and those that he was connected to already had his book.

I was proud of Tyrone, he had most of the tools to be successful, but the key component he was missing was a strategy. He had been doing what worked, never taking time to analyze what was working and why.

For Tyrone, I was able to create a social media campaign for him to execute. I showed him how to repurpose material that he already had in order to give his online followers a fresh look and something that they would be willing to share with their networks. Tyrone was surprised with the impact that just a few minor adjustments made. His books sold better as a result of increasing his fan base. I will address social media as an effective tool in a later chapter.

As you can see the approach for two authors was very different but yielded the same result. It doesn't matter where you are in your literary career or marketing campaign, it's not too late to implement or improve your current plan. The key is to have a plan!

Most authors write with the intent of being a bestseller and dream of that big break. There is a fallacy that, *"if my book could just get into the hands of the most popular radio or television personality then my book sales will sky rocket."* It doesn't do anyone any good to get your book to the perfect media personality if the person is unwilling to read it, nor has any idea where their fans can purchase a copy. Besides, you aren't the only writer that thought of that route of celebrity endorsement so the competition is stiff.

Very few authors take the time to learn about the industry of writing and/or publishing. As I said previously, no matter which publishing option you choose, marketing and promoting your book still has to take place. You can't release a book on Monday and expect to be a best-seller a week later.

The literary community has become overly saturated with books, which means being visible and relevant is a requirement! It doesn't matter where you promote your book. What matters, is that people can find you and refer people to your works.

Being a writer is a business and your books are your product, which means you want to produce and market a product that will make people want to purchase repeatedly and tell others about it. Although being an author requires you to hustle, selling books should not be your hustle, it's a business. If you are simply interested in peddling books, you won't be successful and this is why. An author has to know who his or her target market is in order to successfully reach them.

You may hear people say everyone is your customer. That is simply not true. Some people like romance, while others enjoy science fiction. Some people do not read fiction books at all. If you don't know who you are trying to reach, how do you know what it takes to reach them? Your entire marketing strategy will be based on who your target audience is.

The world is changing daily and it is changing faster than ever before so it's vital that you keep up. I say that to say don't limit your book to just paper back. When applicable you may want to consider eBook, audiobook and languages other than English as options.

Here's a moment of transparency for you. I decided to write my book *You! Branding Yourself for Success* because I had so many people asking me about how I built my brand. I published it in two formats, paperback and eBook. Over a six month period of time, I only sold about 100 copies online. Later, I decided to release the audiobook. I sold 100 copies within the first couple weeks with virtually no advertising.

Based on the feedback that I received, people enjoyed the option to listen, take notes and revisit particular parts of the book. They were able to listen to the book as they were commuting or performing other tasks. I will be honest, by giving readers format options you won't be leaving money on table.

I know marketing may not be a strong suit for a lot of authors, which may be one of the reasons that you chose to write instead of sell. But, it is important to be visible, available and approachable. If you don't want to meet people and actively promote your book, you better have amazing copy and branding collateral that is second to none. Be prepared to flood cyberspace and/or have a responsive mailing list. In a later chapter, I will go more in depth about ways to market your book and be visible.

In the **Write and Grow Rich** courses, I provide you with the opportunity to not only learn how identify your target market, but what they value and how to reach them. So if you are unclear about how to apply any of tools that you have been equipped with in this book, don't be afraid to register for my online or home study courses.

Literary marketing requires consistency, focus and work! No one is going to invite you to be become a famous author or give you a chance *just because.* You have to take a chance on your purpose and find your own seat at the table.

Every successful author you meet will tell you they've endured more than their fair share of challenges, but it was for the love of the pen or the passion of what they had to say that kept them going despite the odds being stacked against them. And yes, that includes me! Yes, there have been times when I questioned if I was a good fit in the literary world and I doubted myself as an author. But every time, I considered throwing in the towel, I would receive a voicemail, email or some form of communication from someone that one of my books helped, inspired, educated or entertained.

I have read books that rendered useless, outdated or too little information about being a successful author. I didn't have a literary mentor or a clear understanding of what being an author was all about. With that being said, I misused marketing dollars, wasted my time at various book signings and was told NO on more occasions than I care to remember. But, I never stopped pursuing my passion for writing and reaching people. And, neither should you!

Every time you think of an excuse to quit, I assure you that you will find a reason to keep going. Your passion for the craft will always draw you back in.

ACTION ITEMS

1. Who do you plan to market your book to? Will it be to the general public or certain organizations?

2. What is your plan to market your book? Is an online campaign or traditional marketing method your best option?

3. Can you market your book on your own or do you need the assistance of a professional?

NOTES

NOTES

NOTES

NOTES

Deondriea Cantrice

Be There or Be Square

With the turn of every corner, there is an eBlast, invitation, mailer, an opportunity to purchase an ad, become a sponsor, participate in a book signing, or a vendor opportunity. How do you make heads or tails of it all? It is sometimes difficult to determine which option will be a lucrative venture for you and the success of your book(s).

Let's start with the fact that cost and value are not synonymous. When planning which events you are willing to participate in, cost should not be the deciding factor no matter how tight your budget may seem. Believe me, free is sometimes more costly than you think. Although cost *is* a factor, it should not be the deciding factor. Your focus should be on the value of the event. You have to ask yourself, what is the anticipated return on your investment (ROI)? Is the investment of time and money worth the possible return?

In order to determine the value of the venture, you have to determine what is your expected return? Are you looking for exposure? Are you seeking the experience of a book signing because you never attended one? Are you looking to sell a predetermined amount of books? Are you simply going because the event is at a good cost on a day that you have nothing else to do? These are questions that no one can answer but you. These questions must be asked and answered prior to signing the contract or agreeing to participate. Once you know the answers to those questions, it will be easier for you to make a decision on which event is right for you.

You may be invited to set up a table at an event to sell your book. Although there was not a fee for you to be there, you may sit at the event for hours and there may only be a handful of people attending this event. Ultimately, you don't sell a single book. How much is your time worth? Did you make contacts with potential and future customers and/or partners? How much promotional material did you pass out?

Also, you can attend an event that has a high registration fee, and still no one shows up. Conversely, with both scenarios you may sell out. The last scenario is that you may sell out and the author next to you may sell nothing at all or vice versa. As you can see it is more than a numbers game.

There are a variety of variables that make some events more successful than others. One of the variables comes down to simple event planning.

- What's the reputation of the venue?

- What is the location of the venue?

- Is the venue easily accessible?

- Is the parking free?

- What other events are going on in the area that may impact the traffic flow?

- What time of day or date is the event?

- How has the event been marketed?

- What other authors or types of authors will be there?

- How many authors will be present?

- Will there be "featured" authors?

- How do I become one of the featured authors?

I know you are thinking to yourself, how am I supposed to know these things and why should I care? The above mentioned variables will affect the foot traffic at the event and ultimately impact the number of potential customers in attendance. Customers are less likely to attend an event when the parking is bad, costly, or inconvenient in any way.

If attendees have to pay entry fees to attend the event, they are less likely to spend additional money with vendors or reduce the amount of money the attendees intended on spending. No matter how much you market, you have to know what you are dealing with. We will discuss marketing and promotions in a later chapter.

Believe it or not, it's not other "book" events that are your event's competition. If the playoffs or a big championship game is on or in the area, even if readers are not sports fans, you can expect people not to show up in high numbers. When planning an event or attending an event, childcare and finances are factors. For example, if a reader can't secure childcare because the people they rely on are attending events themselves. Or the majority of their disposable income is already spent. You are setting yourself up to with the possibility of no or minimal foot traffic at your event.

A perfect example is you may not necessarily want to have a book signing on Super Bowl Sunday. Avid readers may not care about who is playing in the game, but they may be very interested in attending the party with friends, family or significant others. If marketed correctly, a book signing, Super Bowl party can be prosperous. After all, your friends and family will be together in one place. Again, make sure you plan, market and have permission before packing up books to sell at someone else's event.

A couple of years ago a well-known speaker that was notorious for speaking in front of sold out crowds, filled less than half of the arena. The speaker's name alone was enough to draw attention to this event. What went wrong? Well, the speaker was booked downtown (where parking costs), on a Friday (when bars are full), during a holiday weekend. Traffic was horrible, attendees had to fight rush hour traffic, tourists, and people celebrating only to find that the parking was scarce and overwhelmingly expensive. Although the event was free, it was costly in terms of people's time and patience. You run the same risk when it's difficult for people to get to you.

Every business, organization and event is looking to make money directly or indirectly. Money is raised directly when a fee is required to participate, sponsor, attend or partner with the event. Usually the event host makes its money from your participation, regardless if the event is a success or not. For example, a venue may charge the host $250 for the space for the allotted time frame. In turn the host will charge 10 authors $100 for a table at the event. The host has already generated $1,000 in revenue with little work or assuming much risk. That means the host has already made a profit, and doesn't have much of a vested interest in the number of patrons attending the event. You will find that little to no promoting for the event is done. The host will usually depend on the participants to do most, if not all of the marketing.

Indirect revenue may be generated by a fee charged to the attendees and the success of the event is usually predicated by the appearance of a well-known special personality or events. Of course the more people they can get in the room, the more profitable the event will be. In that case, they will promote the event heavily which will create more foot traffic.

There are qualifying questions to ask the event host before you decide if participating is a wise decision for you. Don't be afraid to ask questions, a real business person will anticipate and welcome your questions. You are entitled to receive as much information as you require in making a sound business decision. If a host is reluctant to share this information with you, or becomes agitated because you are asking questions, it is usually an indication that this may not be the event for you. Ask questions and expect them to be answered. If the answer is questionable, follow your gut instinct and back away from the offer.

Here is a set of questions to get you started. Depending on the circumstances of the event you may want to add to the list of questions or omit a few of the questions.

- Is this a first time event?

- What was the result of past events?

- What is the demographic of the attendees?

- What is the anticipated number of attendees?

- How many other vendors will be present?
- Will other authors be represented? If so how many?
- What genres do the other authors represent?
- What are some of the items being sold by the other vendors?
- Where and how has the event been advertised?
- How are the vendor logistics at the event determined?
- What does the vendor/author registration fee include?
- Who are the other event sponsors?
- Do you need to provide your own table and/or chair?
- If the event is outdoors, are tents provided? If not can you bring your own?
- What is the cancellation/refund policy?

It is important that you perform the proper due diligence at the onset, rather than having buyer's remorse afterwards. Whether the fee was $0 or $1m, you have to consider the ROI. What is your fee paying for? Will the event give you exposure? Will you make valuable connections? And of course, will the event generate sales?

No matter what type of publishing option you selected, the profit margin on book sales is not very high. Let's have a simple math lesson. If you decide to accept a local vendor opportunity that costs $100 for you to participate and your book retails for $10, that means you have to sell at least 10 books to break even. Also, it is important that you understand selling 10 books would be your gross profit, not your net profit. Remember you had to purchase the books to sell, and you probably spent money on promotional material, travel, and meals as well.

Don't be afraid to speak to other authors. Ask if they have attended the event in the past and what was his or her experience. Again, this is just *one* variable. We all measure success and failure differently. One author may sell out, whereas the author right next to him or her may have sold nothing at all. One author may have sold 20 books but his or her expectation may have been to sell 50 books.

When you speak to authors about the various events, book fairs and conferences, be very specific with your questions. Why do they feel the way that they do about the event? And, it's okay to ask for the opinion of more than one author/vendor.

One of the key points I want to leave you with is know the audience and venue. For example, if you write street literature you may not want to attempt to sell your books at a metaphysical conference. Also, you may not want to purchase a booth at a hair dresser's conference because most hairdressers are not avid readers, although their clients may be. You may connect with the hairdressers to set up a book signing at his or her shop.

As I said earlier, this is more than a numbers game. Research, weigh yours options, consider the cost, and make a decision that is right for you. The key to determine if an event is right for you is to do your homework on the front end so you don't have to pay on the back end.

Podcasts, Internet radio and Blogtalk Radio are becoming more and more popular. For some it may be the way to go. But, this may not be an obvious choice for all authors. Before agreeing to appear on a show, listen to a couple of the archived episodes to determine the flow of the show, if it is the right platform for you and your book(s) and whether they represent your brand. Not all exposure is good exposure. When appearing on someone's show, ask yourself is the show in alignment with your brand? What are the demographics of their fan base? It's important to know who and what you are dealing with.

Especially as a new author, I know there may be a sense that you have no right to turn down opportunities that are presented to you. You are in control of your marketing strategy; you reserve the right to be selective. You have to know what works for you and will assist you achieving the goals that you desire.

Don't allow anyone to guilt you in appearing anywhere that is not going to present you in the best light. For example, I was invited to have a booth at a knitter's event, with a portion of the event's proceeds to be allocated to a local charity. Of course I was excited about the event and I have a soft spot for charity.

I sat at the event for four hours being avoided like I was in quarantine. Well, knitters are kinesthetic people. They prefer to be busy crafting instead of holding a book. They were especially uninterested in a book that had nothing to do with knitting or crafts. That was a lesson that I only had to be introduced to once in order to grasp.

As you and your works become known, it's ok to mix and match your appearances. You may have budget constraints in the beginning and focus on appearing on podcasts. But, as you become more popular with readers, you may discover live events yield a higher return.

Once readers know you and become more familiar with your work, you will find yourself being invited to various events where the person or book club is willing to pay for all or some of your expenses to make an appearance. Until you reach that plateau, it's important to know your budget, how far you are willing to travel and for how long.

If nothing else, I want you take away from this chapter is to have a plan, conduct your due diligence and know your expected outcome. I guarantee that you will discover what events and invitations yield the best results for you and what you are trying to accomplish with your book(s).

ACTION ITEMS

1. What do you expect to receive from a book signing?

2. How many books or what dollar amount do you plan to sell?

3. Is this event a good use of your time and/or resources?

4. How will you measure your success from this event?

NOTES

NOTES

NOTES

NOTES

Making Dollars and Sense

Now that I have laid the foundation and you have an idea of what you want to do, now it's time to learn how to get there. As I said earlier, there is no silver bullet or magic pill. In fact, no two authors will tell you the same story about how they became a successful, bestselling author. You have to discover what works for you and align with your goals.

In this chapter I will discuss a variety of ways that you can promote yourself, your book(s) and in some cases leverage your books to establish yourself as a subject matter expert. Your marketing success depends solely on how much time, money and other resources that you are willing to invest. Even if you have a manager or publicist, this chapter will be useful to you to help gauge how effective your marketing campaign is or it may introduce you to new strategies.

There are so many outlets to build an audience and promote your books. There is print media, social media, presentations, appearance, speaking engagements, and more. I know that this may seem a little repetitive, but it's imperative that you are equipped with not just the tools of the trade, but how to use them effectively. I'm getting into the reason that you purchased this book.

Let's begin with your brand. Whether you built it or it was handed to you, believe it or not you have a brand. It is important that you protect that brand because it is who you are, what you do, and it's your legacy. That is why it's important to be consistent in everything you do.

Mystery writer? Erotic writer? Christian Fiction writer? Did a name of a specific author or authors immediately come to mind when you read those phrases? Those authors that came to mind have branded themselves so well that they have become synonymous with what they write.

Personal Branding is defined as *the unique promise of value; it is to authenticate yourself in order to establish trust and distinction.* A successful brand has a few significant components used to differentiate goods or services from each other and to help create associations in the minds of consumers that lead to awareness, preference and ultimately choosing your books.

In short, branding is establishing a place to inhabit in the mind of the audience that you encounter and/or are trying to reach. Branding, much like social media, is about making a full-time commitment to the art of defining yourself as a leader in the literary world. Your brand is the total experience of someone reading your books and what you represent as an author.

Branding and marketing are often confused as being the same thing. But they are two separate entities that work in tandem to produce the results that you desire. Branding is the experience and marketing is the method of which you deliver your message.

Marketing is Communicating Your Message to Bring About a Targeted Action

In developing a marketing campaign, don't be afraid to experiment with the different strategies and combine them in a manner that works for YOU! You can choose to roll out several of the techniques in a truncated cycle. The key is to be consistent with your marketing efforts and be patient when looking for the results of your campaign.

What does it take to market your book effectively? I am prepared to provide you with the various tools that you can use to build an effective campaign to promote yourself and market your book.

Marketing Tools

AUTHOR BIO

An author bio is a MUST HAVE! The purpose of a biography, more commonly referred to as a "bio" is a snap shot or executive summary of who you are, what you have accomplished, and what matters to you. In general, your bio should be no more than a single page and should be a balance of who you are personally and professionally.

I know the immediate desire is to cite your accolades in your introduction/bio but remember "added value" is what matters most. How is what is said in your bio valuable to the audience?

What value do you bring? i.e., experiences, connections, track record, and attributes?

Your bio should read verbatim no matter where a person checks. Your bio should be consistent. I recommend that you create both a short (100 words or less) and a full version of your bio (no longer than 1 page.) Your bio should tell a person what you are all about and more importantly, who you are. By sharing a balance of who you are as a person, as well as a snapshot of your accomplishments, people feel like they can connect with you and trust that you know what you are talking about.

It is essential to keep your bio clean and to the point, leaving nothing that needs an explanation. No need to tell where you grew up, your best friend's name, or what you like to do for fun unless it is relevant to your book. On the other side of that, your bio should reflect not mirror your resume. Don't simply list every single award, degree, certification, accolade etc. that you ever received. Just share enough that the audience trusts that you know what you are talking about, but not so much that it overwhelms the audience.

Your bio should include the most important and or recent accomplishments. For example, a singer won a Grammy, which means it's not necessary to list that he or she won first place in the high school talent show. Don't get me wrong, you can speak or write about your accomplishments and everything you've accomplished, just don't overkill the audience with praise and thoughts of grandeur about yourself.

An author hired me to help her create a marketing campaign for her book. I performed a few Internet searches to assess her current strategy and to determine where the holes existed. I researched her online and everywhere I looked her bio read differently. Not only was it different, it was contradictory. The author's book was about surviving domestic violence. One of her bios mentioned that her husband abandoned their marriage. But another bio read that she escaped domestic violence through the support of her family and friends.

Without knowing her story, you would ask yourself what is the truth? What really happened? This minor discrepancy challenged her credibility and the validity of her experience. Her audience may have doubts in their mind. Was she really a battered wife, or was she writing about a "hot topic"?

I asked her about what I read. She explained to me that she packed up her kids, what she could carry and moved escaped the situation of domestic abuse. After which she never heard from him again. Eventually she was granted a divorce based on abandonment because her husband was not able to be located.

As you can see the information was accurate, but because of the inconsistency of how it was presented, it seemed as though she made up the story to fit the arena she was in at the time.

I helped the author draft a one-page bio and showed her how to cut it to fit the requirements of a shorter bio without changing the story.

After living more than a decade in a progressively abusive marriage, Monica decided the safety of her children was her only priority. She gained the courage to escape her abusive marriage. As a survivor, she has made it her mission to empower and equip women with the resources to be victorious after abuse.

By sharing her experience instead of her credentials, it incites interest in what she has to say, with the belief that she would deliver a relatable message instead of rattling off statistics and case studies.

It is important to know your audience and the nature of the event. For example, if she was being cited as an expert in the field of domestic violence to move a bill or get funding for a cause or charity, her 50 word bio would read as follows.

As a domestic abuse survivor, Monica earned a Masters in Psychology and is serving as director of "said agency" for the past 5 years, with a 76% success rate of helping women rebuild their lives. She has raised an excess of $1.3M for families in need.

Although the bios differ in reflecting what she has done and why she has chosen to do it, they both are a modified snapshot designed to reach her target audience and add validity to her knowledge of the subject matter. With it, she has the opportunity to support her cause, rather than explain who she is.

When you are asked for a bio you have two options, send your complete bio and tell the recipient to use as much or as little as they see fit, or craft your own 50 word or less bio.

I know you are a writer, but don't be afraid to hire a copy editor or speech writer to create your bio for you. You can repurpose or edit it as needed. Your profile on the social media platforms should be a derivative of your bio. This will create congruency. No matter where a person searches, they are discovering the same information about you.

MEDIA KIT/PRESS KIT

I know that many of us were taught not to brag. I like to think of promoting yourself as branding not bragging. Having a media kit is your moment to shine and put your best foot forward. This is your moment to showcase yourself and your work.

By having a media kit, you are prepared to present yourself and/or your book(s) in a consistent, well executed manner. Your media kit is not just for the 'media." A media kit is a *pre-packaged set of promotional materials of a person, company, or organization and distributed for the purpose of press, introduction or other announcements.*

How you package yourself will set the precedence of how you are viewed by others. Your media kit should be prepared, consistent and readily available. Your media kit should contain the items that are applicable to the audience that you are trying to reach. My media kit contains a personalized introduction letter when necessary, my bio, promotional material like postcards, a sales slick, bookmarks, infographics, and/or a DVD. These items are neatly arranged in a customized folder. Depending on who I am sending the media kit and why, I will also include a copy of my book.

It's a good idea to develop an *electronic press kit* (EPK) and have it readily available for email and a link to the PDF copy on your website. By always being prepared, you don't have to waste valuable time getting prepared.

I know you are thinking what is the difference between a bio and a media kit? Your media kit is what you look like, sound like, (when applicable), what your books are about, what people are saying about you, and who you are as an artist. You don't want to appear too vague or ambiguous, but you also don't want to waste a reader's time with an avalanche of interesting yet useless facts about your life. Include personal information, but only as it relates to you as an author. It should be a 1-page PDF document with your intro paragraph including your current information, what you are promoting, with a chronological account of your recent news or accomplishments.

While your bio is a cornerstone of an EPK, your bio also has its own purpose. If you are going to be interviewed or if someone is making an introduction on your behalf, your bio is extremely helpful for them to have beforehand. It is also a key way for fans to learn more and connect with you. Your bio should have its own page on your website, as well as a link for visitors to download. Key information from your bio should be contained within your social media profiles as well.

COPIES OF YOUR BOOK

Your book is one of the best physical pieces of collateral that you own. Use it! What better way to grasp the attention of someone than with the book itself. Mailing your book to prominent, interested readers, sponsors and the media serves as an excellent calling card. I know that the books cost you, but don't be afraid to give them away. It is essential that you possess a strategic plan. Develop a list of people that you believe will be interested in your book and send advanced copies for review, donated copies for giveaways, or as a part of your media kit.

Copies of your book can also be given away to winners of contests. I will discuss contests in more depth later in this book. However, people love winning and winning your book is another way to gain more press. People will definitely share what they won to anyone that will listen, especially if you package it well.

PRESS RELEASES

Whenever you have a new release or upcoming event, it is a good idea to craft and distribute a press release to the media, your email contacts, and on all social media platforms. A lot of times people are able and willing to support you and your works, but they aren't able to if they don't know what's going on. Sending out a press release may be a little uncomfortable in the beginning because conceptually you may feel like you are bragging. Let me dispel that by saying its advertising! All you are doing is letting others know what you are doing.

I recommend using both digital and print marketing efforts when sending out a press release. By casting a large and wide net, you are destined to capture the attention of more people. In this particular scenario, more is better.

REVIEWS/TESTIMONIALS

Getting reviews about your book is a great way to promote your book. I know you may be a little nervous about a stranger critiquing your work. You have poured your heart and soul into crafting the perfect book and the last thing you want is running the risk of someone telling you that they don't like it or something is wrong with it. Don't let that reason hold you back from encouraging others to review your book.

Most reviewers are professionals and they don't let their personal biases interfere with their assessment of your work. Even if the review is less than favorable, if it is well written it will not hinder readers from purchasing your book(s). Yes, you run the risk of receiving a few negative reviews, but you also have the opportunity to receive several good reviews.

A review gives a reader a glimpse into your works and what to expect from you as a writer. Even with an unfavorable review readers will still purchase your book with an expectation. Think about it, how many movies have you enjoyed that the critics hated? Does their opinion carry a lot of weight with you? Probably not. People view everything through their own lens. In fact, most people want to judge things for themselves.

Another benefit of a review is it will also assist you in improving your writing ability, if you take heed to the advice. When I published my first book, I submitted it to a reviewer that had a reputation of being the harshest in the industry. She gave me a less than favorable review but it was very positive feedback for me. I took everything she said to heart when I sat down to craft my second book. And yes, it worked! I have not received anything less than a four star review on my second book. I will go a step further; my second book improved the sales of my first book.

A review whether good or bad creates buzz about your book and that is what you want. The more places and frequency your title appears, the easier it will be for readers to discover you and find your book(s). Make sure your book is as visible as possible.

If your book is nonfiction, it is a great idea to get testimonials from people that have read your book and/or applied its principles. People sometimes like to know what others experienced before they try it. Testimonials are a great way to establish yourself as a subject matter expert.

Reviews and testimonials alike can be repurposed. Both of these items can be posted on your various social media platforms or as a part of your promotional packages. You telling people how great your book is may be considered as bragging but someone else talking about it is known as branding.

PICTURES/VIDEOS

You know how the saying goes, "a picture is worth a thousand words." We have become a visual society. If you don't believe me, ask the advertisers that spend millions of dollars each year for a 30-60 second television commercial. Posting pictures of your book and events is a great way to connect with readers. As I said earlier, an eye catching book cover makes the difference between your book being picked up or overlooked.

By visually promoting your book, readers will become familiar with you and your works and it becomes a more enticing read. Capturing pictures of your various events with readers and other authors is extremely engaging. People will welcome, enjoy and share their 15 minutes of fame with you. Pictures and videos can be used to inform, educate, or excite readers about your book(s). Create a Book Trailer about your book. A book trailer is similar to a movie trailer. It is a teaser or a snapshot into your book. The dramatization will help sell the plot of your book. A video trailer of your book is a way to draw readers in, giving them a vivid look inside your story.

INTERVIEWS

Making in person, radio, Internet or print interviews is a great way to gain exposure and expand your audience. Personally, what I love about interviews is the promotion efforts are doubled. The publication, entity or person that is doing the interview will advertise your appearance and they already have an established fan base. If you are invited to be interviewed, you or your book is of interest to the host and the audience that you are being exposed to. This is useful because you are being granted access to a target market with essentially no effort.

Whether fiction or non-fiction, readers enjoy hearing about what you have in store. What better person to tell about the book than the person that wrote it. After all, you should have given some thought to who your ideal audience was when you began to pen your book. Although we all strive to become a best seller, not everyone is within your target market.

Don't rely solely on the interviewer to promote you. I know its "their" event, show or venue. However, if you have a fan base as well that is interested in what you have going on and is interested in sharing you and your book(s) with their connections. You would be doing yourself a great disservice if you failed to promote yourself in conjunction with the efforts of the interviewer.

TOUR SCHEDULE

Posting your tour schedule on your website is a great way to attract readers. When readers know that you are personable and in demand that will entice them to jump on the bandwagon so to speak. Whether a fan already has your book or is new to your works, they welcome the opportunity to meet you and learn more about you.

Virtual tour and in person appearances are equally effective if marketed properly. I'm sure it's your desire to be nationally and internationally known, which means not all fans will have the opportunity to meet you in person right away. Virtual tours are a way to include fans that can't reach attend one of your appearances in person. Also, they are inexpensive and saves you time.

It is important to keep your tour schedule updated, and it's ok to leave one or two previous events in addition to your upcoming appearances on your website, no matter how far in the future they are.

It is just as important to post your appearances on all of your social media platforms because it makes it easier for people to share your event with their networks. I will go more in depth about leveraging social media when I reach the social media marketing portion of this book.

PROMOTIONAL MATERIAL

As an author, you are in the business of selling your books. It is important that you conduct your business accordingly. Promotional material is not your brand, but it does reflect your brand. If you don't believe promotional material is important, look around your immediate area and count how many logos or brands that you see. Sitting here typing, I see more than 20 different brand logos.

Most writers say that they are not "sales people." Promotional material is a way for you to sell your book without having to "sell." There are several items that you can purchase as promotional material, such as postcards, bookmarks, t-shirts, pens, flyers, banners, so on and so forth. Every author should have a limitless supply of some if not all of these products. The purpose of promotional material is to allow you to leave an impression or solicit an invitation from readers.

Personally, I am a shopaholic so I buy a variety of promotional materials and use them differently. I use bookmarks in lieu of business cards. Yes, I have business cards also but when I am at a book signing or I'm giving away promotional items bookmarks are the best choice. The average person will throw away a business card or add your name to their database, but they will generally hold on to a bookmark even if they are not an avid reader. Not to mention that bookmarks are very inexpensive.

Promotional material is a personal decision. It depends on how much you want to spend, the genre of your book and your target audience. Whatever promotional material you decide to purchase there are a few things to keep in mind. Keep the promotional material consistent. Let me repeat that again. Brand consistency is key! If your bookmarks are black and blue, your banner should not be red and white.

When people see your promotional material, they need to have a level of expectation. Inconsistency gives a sense of confusion and that is not what you want people to feel when they see your brand. The only color variance should be a colored logo or picture and a black and white, also referred to as a greyscale. The greyscale image is perfect for ads that are being printed in black and white. Sometimes a color print will copy too dark or look grainy.

The other important component necessary for your promotional material is have your contact information on your promotional material. It is essential that you add the BEST contact information. What does that mean? If you are not a person that keeps a consistent telephone number or choose not to have people reach you by phone, then do not add your telephone number. If you are not a social media person, do not indicate where people can find you online.

There is nothing worse than putting incorrect information on your promotional material. I actually sat beside an author who scratched out her information on her bookmarks prior to the show and handwrote the updated information. We both watched as people picked up her bookmarks, read them and put them back down. Needless to say she did not sell very many books either. Before going to print, make sure you proof it, have a second set of eyes review it, and verify the information again.

Promotional material is purchased with the intent to give away, so give away things that people are most likely to hold on to for a while. I avoid disposable items like candy and water bottles because they will be discarded after they are used. Think about it, how will your name or the name of your book resonate with the reader if that immediately discarded the item that you gave him or her?

Promotional material is a personal preference, just make sure you have some that accurately reflects your brand, contains contact information and is consistent. In a nutshell, promotional material is the best way to touch the senses of your target audience through more than one avenue.

ONLINE PRESENCE

With the continual advancement of and evolution of technology, the ability to reach your fan base and target audience around the clock is at your fingertips. Creating and fostering an online presence is a great avenue to network, sell, and promote yourself and your works effortlessly. You don't have to speak "geek" in order to have an active sustainable online presence.

Websites

It is a good idea to have an author website. The most novice person can navigate themselves to a website with ease. I know that social media platforms are what most people want to gravitate to when it comes to having an online presence, but a website is a low maintenance approach in establishing your cyber footprint.

There are several different options for building a great website. There are a variety of outlets that offer do-it-yourself templates to create your website. Or, you can always hire a web designer to build the website for you.

The benefit of having a website is it gives the general public access to you without having to join or subscribe to an online platform that you don't control or own. Websites also serve as the cornerstone of your online presence. From your website you can add pictures, videos and links to your other online platforms. Also, most web addresses are not blocked by firewalls.

Websites are low maintenance. There is not a need to make continuous content updates, except for event dates and other real time information that you would like to share. Unlike social media platforms, a website is to push information to your audience rather than exchange information with your audience.

Social Media

Social media is defined as *any and all online interaction, creation or exchange online between you and people in cyberspace*. Yes, that includes all social media platforms, blogs, websites, online portfolios, Internet radio, really simple syndication (RSS), webinars and even online surveys.

There are a variety of online platforms designed to share things such as common interests, communities, relationships, and other demographics amongst users. The advantage of social media is that you are using technology, interconnectivity, and relationships to form new bonds between individuals and strengthen old ones.

Social networking is also based on understanding social media and power of the connections, and then leveraging them to create even stronger relationships. The ultimate value of social networking sites is to develop a database and connect with people who have similar interests.

Take the time to understand and research the various platforms and networks for your clientele (your target market) to determine which ones are right for you. If you are not already active online, I suggest that you sign up with several to determine which platforms are the most effective and cross- pollinate.

One of the best advantages of social media is that it provides you with the opportunity to cast a wide and vast net to mine for your ideal readers for little to no cost. Because of the structure of social media, you are afforded the opportunity to reach the networks of the people that you are connected to. A simple post will connect you to the networks of the people that you are associated with.

I would be remiss if I didn't convey to you that social media can be your best friend or your worst enemy. The fact that social media is real-time is a double-edged sword. The advantage of social media being real-time is that you immediately can see what your fan base and target market responds to and is currently discussing. The disadvantage of social media being a real-time outlet is that your reputation can be destroyed in the blink of an eye if your social media campaign is not managed properly. You don't have to fear the paparazzi when society is flooded with camera phones.

Let me address a few do's and don'ts of social media.

DO:

Be consistent-It is important that your social media campaign is congruent with your brand. I cannot express how important consistency is.

Be engaging-Create content that will prompt people to interact and respond to you. The key is to have content that readers find valuable.

Be interactive-The key to an effective social media campaign is to develop a dialogue with your fan base. There should be an exchange, not just you pushing information to readers. Through this interaction readers will have a sense of belonging.

Follow others-There is a fallacy to only support those who support those who support you. WRONG! When you connect with others online and like, comment and share their posts and tweets, it exposes you to their fan base. I cannot express how many fans I gathered by simply engaging in a conversation on someone else's page. Remember other authors, editors, reviewers, and publishers etc. attract readers and that is who you want to connect with.

Utilize several platforms/methods-Although you may have a platform that you are most comfortable with don't be afraid to cross pollenate your content. You may post a picture on Facebook but tweet the message, or create a video message.

DON'T

Shamelessly self-promote-When you are interacting with others providing content that people deem valuable it will attract the people that you are trying to reach. Unless invited to, don't post your URLs or promote yourself on someone else's page or thread.

Hashtag Abuse-Using hashtags is a great strategy for SEO ranking, but only use words that people are likely to search unless it is a brand building hashtag. For example I use #authorpreneur to build my brand as an author. But I would not post the following: *"up #late my #creative #juices are #flowing #writing this #chapter. #mygrindneverstops* The overuse of hashtags makes your sentence difficult to read and will not improve your SEO ranking.

Tag Abuse-Unless you have permission of someone or the information is pertinent to the person don't tag them in your posts. Some people may find tagging without permission offensive, while some of your fans may feel excluded because he or she was not tagged in the post.

Ignore comments- It does take a lot of time to effectively manage a social media campaign. But it's essential that you acknowledge comments in a timely manner. Not only will it make the reader feel important, but it will also improve your visibility through the use of the behind the scenes *algorithms*. In my workshops, I teach a module on time management techniques and social media.

Literally, I can draft an entire book on my success as an author using social media, but I will save that for my course. I don't want you to become overwhelmed or obsessed with your social media presence and you miss the other gems in this book.

Another benefit of social media is there are a variety of tools that you can utilize that will assist you in automating some of your posts. Don't look at social media an additional task that you have to develop new content for, repurpose the information that you already have.

Blogging

A web log, also known as a blog is a great way to increase your exposure. Blogging is regular written or video entries of less than 1000 words about a particular subject or theme. These brief snapshots known as blog posts are a way to gain the interest of your target market and develop a loyal following.

Blogging serves as a teaser or a sample of your writing style to readers. Your blog gives readers a taste of what they have to look forward to in your books or subjects that they find interesting. If you are already published, use a blog to share parts of your life or a particular theme of the book. For example, if you write inspirational books, blog about subjects that will encourage, inspire and empower your readers.

If you choose to blog, make sure you are consistent, engaging, interactive, and relevant. This will help you remain in the forefront of the minds of your fan base. And blogging is an additional skill set that you can add to your literary portfolio.

eZine

An electronic magazine (eZine) or newsletter is a valuable marketing tool to promote your works and gain exposure. These gems go hand in hand with a list of interested people that you gather yourself or pay to have developed for you. This list is usually comprised of recipients that you may not be connected with via social media platforms. Your goal is to create a regularly scheduled distribution to your targeted email list. Try to get the recipient's first name and e-mail address so that you can address them by name in the greeting of your eZine. Create content that offers free and valuable teaser articles, excerpted from books or other material you're selling. Once the teaser grabs the reader's attention, you invite them to make a purchase online at your site in order to read the information in its entirety.

Another benefit to having an eZine or newsletter as an active online marketing campaign is you can sell ad space to people and businesses that align with your brand as a way to generate additional income for you, and add value to the publication for your readers.

Speaking engagements

Books can serve as an impulse item at the back of the auditorium where you just finished speaking about a topic from your book, knowledge or experiences. Having a book as supporting material for any topic makes you an "author-ity" on the subject and lends credibility. When news programs are looking for an expert to give their opinion on a hot news item, you or a representative from your company can be that resource on an ongoing basis. They plug you and your book or business on local or national TV/radio. You can save or record those clips to use as promotional pieces. As a frequent guest on a show you may get called by their affiliates and other network shows.

When you're pitching a new product, service, workshop or speaking event, the 50% of listeners who don't sign up may buy a book. They may feel as if they are getting what you offer at a discounted rate, but your marketing just paid off.

Create a seminar or workshop

Depending on the subject of your book, it is a good idea to develop a workshop, seminar or talk based upon your book. Creating a workshop or seminar is a way to generate conversation about your book and increase your credibility. Also a workshop will serve as a marketing tool to gain awareness about your book as well.

Sponsorship

Every day there are events that happen on a local and national level that are always looking for sponsors at a variety of levels. Whether its ad space, meal/speaker sponsorship or giveaways for gift bags, it's a good idea to sponsor events when they are in alignment with your brand. Again, sponsorships will give you exposure to people that you may not normally be able to reach.

Be strategic with the events you sponsor because not every event will be worthwhile. For example if you author street literature, sponsoring a church event may not be the best move. An athletic or any type of kinesthetic focused event may not be a good fit for an author unless your book focuses on health or wellness because most athletes are kinesthetic or auditory learners and reading is usually not high on their to-do list. However, this is why you should offer your book as an audio and/or an eBook, because they can conveniently read as they travel or listen to your book as they workout.

Here are a few questions that you should ask prior to agreeing to a sponsorship.

- *What type of event is it?*
- *What are the demographics of the attendees?*
- *How many attendees are expected?*

There may be times that you want to sponsor an event for strictly charitable purposes like taking an ad out in a high school playbill or donating giveaways. Again, know the purpose and expectation behind your sponsorship.

Always keep a book with you

You never know when you will be faced with an opportunity of a lifetime. It is a good idea to keep at least one copy of your book and media kit with you because you never know who you are going to run into and where.

One evening I attended a networking event a friend of mine was hosting. She was short a door prize for the evening. I offered her a book as a giveaway. When she gave away the book, she asked that I stand and be recognized. As a result, I sold a few copies of my book and scheduled a book signing. What if I didn't have my book with me? There's an old adage that says "stay ready so you don't have to get ready."

Offer your book in different versions

Today, some books transcend across several generations. You can find books that were published several years ago, now being release in an audio format. Some people are old school and prefer the feel of a book in their hands. No matter how tech savvy they may be, there is something about holding an old-fashioned book in their hands that appeals to them. With that being said, it's a good idea to make sure your book is available in hardcover, paperback, eBook, audiobook or any combination thereof.

With every passing day, we are becoming more and more a mobile society. Between commuting and multi-tasking people are on the go more than ever before. To reach some readers your book(s) have to be available in eBook and/or audio form. The cost to transform your book into an eBook is nominal. And, the cost to convert your book into an audio version is well worth the investment. You don't want to alienate any potential readers because of limited version options.

Partner with other authors

I have been very successful when I have had a collaborative book signing with other authors. I know the first thought that may have popped into your mind was, "why invite in the competition?" Well, there is no such thing as competition when you know your purpose. Also, readers are rarely browsers. In most cases they show up with the intent to purchase books, and rest assured they will not only buy your book but the book of your co-host as well.

The benefit of this joint venture is dual advertising. By combining marketing efforts, you are able to extend your reach further than you could if you were working at it alone. Besides, it's great to build connections and allies in the industry. I don't recommend that you partner with other authors because of hidden agendas, but connect with authors for a purpose. It has to be a mutually advantageous venture in order for it to be successful.

Connections/Collaborations

As you can imagine, just like any other career there will be networking opportunities for you. These opportunities can come in the form of collaborations, joint ventures and more. You may be invited to co-author, co-host or even write an article. Like I said in the previous chapter, know what you are willing to invest. Ask yourself, how much of your time and/or resources are you willing to spend before you commit to anything? Once you answer that question, then determine what is or isn't negotiable.

You will discover very quickly that people will want to connect or shall I say attach to you when they see your success. Beware! I know this is going to sound a little arrogant and may make some of you uncomfortable, but if a person isn't doing as well or better than you are, don't partner with them. If they don't offer a specialized skill, expertise or established fan base, don't partner. Always consider how the partnership benefits you. Will the partnership be in alignment with your brand? And, how well will the partnership be received by your readers?

The partnership doesn't have to be an equitable exchange, but it does have to be mutually beneficial. Even though there are millions of writers, the literary community is rather small. You don't want to acquire a bad reputation because of who you are connected to. Nor do you want to build resentment towards the person that you partnered with because he or she didn't deliver what they promised when they promised it. If you choose to partner, be sure to get every aspect of the partnership outlined in writing.

As a writer, your desire is to make money. However, there is nothing wrong with writing for free when it provides other benefits. Although I had already published 4 books when I finally hired a publicist, she struggled on how to package me. Each of my books fell into different genres and my writing resume was extremely shallow. When it came time for her to pitch me to various publications, it was asked, "Well what else has she written?" I had not established a trail so she had to change her strategy of pitching me.

Additionally, if you are looking to establish yourself as a subject matter expert, the more written material you possess, the more invitations you will receive to appear, and the more you can demand as a speaker.

Find Readers

Book Clubs and Literacy groups still exist, but you

have to seek them out. This is where those media kits and copies of your book come in handy. Search the Internet and social media platforms to find them. Once you are in contact with the book club, request permission to mail them a media kit and a complimentary copy of your book.

Reaching out to organized book clubs gives you exposure and it is an opportunity to discuss your book with the club. Readers love that personal interaction. It is very important that you conduct your due diligence prior to contacting the book club or you will be wasting your time and product. It's extremely important to know what genre of books that the club reads. Not all book clubs are into erotica, street literature, sci-fi or inspirational books.

I suggest that you offer book clubs a discounted price on your books because they will usually purchase at least 10 copies. All of the book clubs that I have connected with have welcomed me back with each release. Just like with any business, it is easier and less expensive to maintain clients (readers) than it is to mine for new ones.

Many authors say to me, "I'm not good at advertising and promoting my book." I always respond by saying one or more of the options that I have mentioned in this book will accommodate every personality type and skill level. Also, if you don't feel confident about promoting your book on your own, you can always contract a person that will assist you in effectively promoting your book. They key is to find the combination that best fits you, your book, your budget and your skills.

Lastly, I recommend that you establish who your target market is and be as specific as possible. Is your target audience African-American females between the ages of 25-40? Or Hispanic males 18-24? Or White men over 50? Once you know who you want to market to it will be much easier to create an effective strategy. Let's be realistic, what appeals to a male under 25 will not capture the attention of a woman over 40.

Do not be afraid to contract the services of a publicist or marketing professional to get you started in the right direction. I can assure you that it is well worth the money. Weigh the cost of attempting to market on your own in an ineffective manner versus hiring a professional to at least get you started.

It doesn't matter if you are already published and started on your way, or if you are just beginning. Start from where you are, add and subtract as needed. Remember, this book is a roadmap, it can get you where you're going no matter where your starting point is.

Marketing Checklist

- ❑ Author Biography

- ❑ Author Headshots

- ❑ Author EPK

- ❑ Author Social Media Presence

- ❑ Author Website

- ❑ Author Branding Collateral

- ❑ Author pictures with readers

- ❑ Author videos

- ❑ Author reviews

As I already mentioned, each of these items hold a specific purpose, so it's a good thing to have them all. If you are missing some or all of these items, don't fret! You still have time. If you are working with time and/or budget constraints, I would recommend, the headshot, bio, and social media presence and build from that point on.

The most important take away from this chapter is to be creative and consistent. You never know who is watching you and why.

TO-DO

TO-DO

TO-DO

Press On!

You are a writer! Along with having a book, the opportunity to promote your book(s) through a variety of channels, including the media comes with it. The media includes but is not limited to radio, the Internet, webinars and television. There is a distinct difference between all of those media outlets, but I am going to classify all forms of media as "press" to keep from sounding repetitive.

The press can either be your best friend or worst enemy. An interview can make or break your public image. The only approach to reduce the chances of negative press or a bad interview is to be prepared and leave nothing to chance.

One of the best ways to prepare is to know what you are going to say before you have to say it. Of course there is no way to foresee what questions you will be asked, but you can develop a series of questions of your own just in case you are asked. Many of us don't like talking about ourselves which means when we are asked questions about ourselves, we have a tendency to be uncomfortable and stumble over our words and thoughts if we are not prepared.

Here are a few frequently asked questions that you can practice answering to become more comfortable speaking in an interview and answering questions.

- What is one thing that you would like people to know about you?

- How long have you been writing?

- What inspired you to write this book?

- What is your book about?

- Why should people buy your book?

- What advice would you give aspiring authors?

- Knowing what you know today, what is one thing as an author you would do differently?

- What do you consider to be your greatest feat personally or professionally?

Did you find yourself pausing to search for the answer to some of the questions? If you were giving a live interview, that pause would have been dead air, which is never a good thing when you are on air.

If you have to pause and think, come up with what I like to call your "filler blurb." Your filler blurb is nothing more than something to say as you gather your thoughts. Here are a few of my filler blurbs that I have used with a mild mannered chuckle as I gathered my thoughts:

> *Wow, I wasn't expecting that question.*
> *No one has ever asked me that before.*
> *Let me think about that one.*
> *Is it time for a commercial?*

If you are not comfortable answering a question, with confidence say, *I'm not comfortable with answering that question, I don't answer questions about my personal life,* or some variations thereof. And, feel comfortable enough saying it without offering an explanation. Whatever your response is keep it brief and direct.

Tips for television

More often than not, television and radio interviews are live events and you won't get a "do over." There is no such thing as being *too prepared.* Preparedness is what separates professionals from amateurs. Interviews are a good way to promote your book and if you are a non-fiction writer, interviews will also help establish you as a subject matter expert.

What I enjoy about interviews is it's a no cost way to promote yourself and your book. If you are well equipped for the interview, this will be one of your best opportunities to put you best foot forward.

How do you prepare for an interview? Be prepared for everything! I will discuss preparing for an on camera interview, and then I will discuss radio interviews.

Image is everything. One of the most important elements of being prepared is in preparing how you look or appear on camera. Dress appropriately. Be comfortable and wear outfits that do not take attention away from you or the topic. Make sure you wear clothes that fit appropriately. If your clothes are too big, little, or short, you will fidget throughout the interview. Because you may not know what the set will look like until you arrive, it's a good idea to wear an outfit that you look good in sitting or standing.

It is a good idea to hire an image consultant or stylist prior to your first on air interview to make sure that you are wearing the colors and clothing style that best compliments you. It depends on your personal preference if you want a one-time or ongoing relationship with a stylist. If you aren't in a position to hire someone, I recommend that you wear bright, solid colors that you feel good in. You don't know what the host or other guests may be wearing and you don't want to clash patterns. Other clothing recommendations include:

- Avoid wearing a brand new outfit because you may not be comfortable in it and you do not want your posture or mannerisms to appear as though you are uncomfortable or nervous.
- Choose an outfit that you feel good in. We all have one outfit or color that we wear and we're showered with compliments. Choose that one!
- Always dress professionally unless otherwise appropriate. It is always better to be over dressed than underdressed
- Be a total package because you never know what angle the camera may catch so make sure you are put together from head to toe.

Ladies only

Ladies, if you are not a woman that typically wears makeup; this would be the time to change your beliefs at least for the appearance. You are absolutely welcome to have your own style, but between the camera and the lighting, it's easy to look pale and blend into the set. You don't have to put on so much makeup that your own mother wouldn't recognize you, but just enough to enhance and bring out your features.

If you are a woman that typically wears makeup, you may want to apply it a little heavier than usual especially around the eyes. The lights can flatten your face by removing all the definition. Try not to overdo it because you don't want your makeup to be a distraction. Don't try to compete with theatrical performers by applying too much. You don't want to scare the viewers.

The studio lights can get a bit warm, and on top of being nervous, you don't want to wear too much makeup only to have it run off while you're on camera. The lighting may also cause you to appear a little shiny or cause you to perspire. Blot your face prior to the interview to ensure a cool, calm appearance. Do not use regular tissues or toilet paper. Sometimes they leave pieces stuck to your face. Invest in facial blotting tissues to help reduce sweat and shine.

Gentlemen only

Men, I know that it is easy to assume that you don't have nearly as many grooming requirements as women have. It is true that you have fewer, but your grooming needs are just as, if not more impactful.

Gentlemen, your hair should be neatly cut, your facial hair shaved or trimmed and your clothing neatly pressed. Looking disheveled or like you just rolled out of bed can be very distracting. Whether business or casually dressed, you have to be put together from head to toe. Pay attention to your socks, make sure they are matching, clean and long enough. There is nothing more noticeable than seeing leg instead of sock when a man is seated.

If you are not a suit and tie kind of guy and the interview is more business formal, then a collared shirt and sport coat will do. But no matter what, be comfortable standing as well as sitting without fidgeting.

Other distractions for you, the interviewer and/or audience may be loose change in your pocket, or pockets that are stuffed with a bulky wallet and/or phone. Your pockets should be, if not totally empty, at least empty enough that you can sit comfortably.

Whether male or female, it's a good idea to know the culture and format of the show to make sure your appearance is a match. If the show is a casual setting, dress casually. Business or more formal shows require a more conservative outfit. Inquire as to the audience demographics so you'll understand who is listening or watching and how you can tailor the interview to appeal to their audience.

For some, being in front of the camera can be a little intimidating. You have to be as natural as possible. Do not stare into the camera, focus on your conversation with the interviewer and let the camera operators catch your close-ups. If you watch the camera instead of engaging in the conversation, it may appear that the interview is scripted. The camera crew is trained to capture your interaction.

If possible, outline a few points you would like to discuss with the interviewer prior to the show. If you have your frequently asked questions (FAQs), prepared that should suffice. It's understandable if you are a little nervous, but try not to ramble. Stay focused on the topic and answer the questions as directly as possible. And of course, keep your answers interesting. Try to avoid one-word answers unless it's appropriate.

Be lively and entertaining, but professional. Use vivid words to describe characters and scenes from your book. Or, if your book is non-fiction, address the major points in your book with enthusiasm. Check your voice volume and inflection. Enunciate clearly and speak with confidence and excitement. Your answers, also referred to as "sound-bytes," may be 10, 20 or 30 seconds long and they must be interestingly fascinating and include crucial information about you and your book.

If the interview is by telephone, smile and visualize an audience. Project an enthusiastic personality and image with your voice. Send smiles through the radio waves. If you are asked a question that does not relate to your book, or asked your opinion of another author or something that is off topic, simply say, "I am not sure." Change the subject back to your topic gracefully.

When telling your personal story, make sure it has human interest. Tell a successful or humorous story about how you became an author. Think of a story that the audience can relate to.

Although, you are being interviewed on someone else's platform, the segment is about you, and you have to be comfortable talking about you, your expertise and your book. If you are asked a question that embarrasses you, simply rephrase the question and answer it with tact and grace. By doing this, you will keep the interviewer on topic, and avoid saying something you may regret later. Avoiding interview pitfalls takes practice and a little time to get over the shock, but soon experiences like these roll off your back like a seasoned expert.

Be sure to tactfully plug your upcoming events, appearances and where to purchase your book(s) or products. Above all, be yourself and do not put the interviewer on a pedestal. By the way, don't climb up on one yourself. Never become so arrogant that people don't welcome you. When possible, obtain video, photographs, and/or audio of every interview or speaking engagement for future use and to critique.

Print interviews are much the same, except they can be more comfortable. The interviewer may tape the conversation and write the article from the tape. Carefully answer questions related to other professionals. The media can be unforgiving at times. Read a few editions of the publications to prepare for the type of interviews and articles they print. Review the column of the interviewer or writer to understand their journalistic style. At the end of the interview, ask if contact information can be included in the article and find out how you can get a copy for your records.

The number one rule to remember when you are being interviewed whether in person or print is; do not say anything that can haunt you for the rest of your life. Even when the camera or recorder is off, you can still be quoted for the record.

Internet radio, webinars and video chats are growing in popularity. If you are speaking or being interviewed via one of those mediums, the same rules and practices mentioned above are applicable.

There are some things to consider PRIOR to contacting the media. Educate yourself on various techniques for dealing with the media.

- Develop a media list and update it often.

- Write articles or a column for local media. Create a "tip" or "top ten" article for publication in various newspapers and magazines. Research those that best fit your genre, category or topic and present yourself as an expert on a given topic. As an author, you are considered an "authority" on the topic or genre in which you write. Nonfiction authors feel more secure with this statement than fiction writers, but realize that when you write about things you *know* and get published, you can consider yourself enough of an authority to be taken seriously.

- Send out news releases as often as necessary. Create news releases to include timely and newsworthy information.

- Keep your media kit current at all times.

Now that you have prepared, here is a list of points to ensure that your own personal PR plan stays on track:

- Use proper telephone etiquette and answer each call with a smile. Emotions are detected in your voice. Take detailed messages and return all phone calls, never blowing anyone off. Inquire into the nature of each call and handle accordingly.

- Show appreciation for the business you are given. Let the purchaser(s) know by sending a thank you note. Any publicity you receive or any kind gesture should be followed up with a thank you note.

- Be a person of integrity. If you give your word on anything, make sure you stand by it. Being dependable and accountable is very important; it is evidence of your character. This is vital to the reputation that you build in the industry.

- Take time to listen to whomever you are meeting with. Don't be so eager to respond or make a point. Sometimes not listening can be our biggest downfall.

At one point or another, every athlete has been told by his or her coach, *"you practice like you play."* Or, we are all familiar with the phrase, *"practice makes perfect."* The more you prepare and practice the better outcome you will have. Practice sitting, standing and speaking in front of your mirror and/or someone that will provide you with *honest* feedback. It's up to you to develop a relationship with the media as a friend or a foe. Ultimately be yourself and enjoy the spotlight!

ACTION ITEMS

1. Build a list.

2. Develop a relationship with the contacts on your list.

3. Market to the contacts on your list.

NOTES

NOTES

NOTES

Conclusion

Becoming a well-known, successful author is challenging, but not impossible. I cannot tell you how many aspiring authors have come to me for advice and/or to be mentored and they are surprised when I tell them how much work is required. I'm still not sure what they hope for when they come to me, but I always give them a direct, unclouded view into the literary world.

It takes work, creativity and consistency in order to become a well-known, successful author. It may appear as if authors became an overnight success. The reality is successful authors have been working at it for a while. Readers finally discovered them and spread the word about those authors in what seems to be overnight. The truth is the buzz has been probably going on for a while.

There are several things that I have done right and a few things that I have done wrong that has landed me where I am today. I have been known to fail gracefully after signing up for events or sponsorships that left me holding an empty bag.

I even took a three year hiatus from writing because I was "burnt out." Through self-examination I discovered that I was burnt out from writing, it was being a one "woman show" had taken its toll on me. I was the management and talent. Before I knew it, I was all management and no talent. In other words, I searched for and booked all of my book signings, appearances and interviews. I was my own accountant and secretary. With the exception of having a graphic designer, I was doing everything on my own, which left little time for what I truly loved which is writing. Yes I juggled all those balls, but not effectively. And, it wasn't until I began to delegate some of my responsibilities that I became more successful.

I had to come up with a plan and contract people to help me execute that plan, people whose core competencies were different than mine. Yes, it was a hard pill to swallow to pay someone to complete tasks that I could do on my own. But hiring a copy editor for example, was money that was well spent, because it saved me time and helped me narrow my focus. By narrowing my focus, my mind was clearer and as a result of a clear mind, I was able to write more freely and ultimately attracted more readers.

Before I offer advice to aspiring authors, I ask him or her to clearly define what success means to them, what it looks like, and what it feels like. Success is different for everyone. You cannot compare where other authors are and what they are doing to your own activities and success.

Watching others will cause you to lose sight of your own goals and will only lead you in circles. I will say, if you want to adopt some of the best practices from other authors that's fine. But, don't judge your success based on other author's perceived success, especially if you don't know what it took for them to get where they are.

Here are a few pieces of advice that I share with aspiring authors when I am contacted.

If you desire to be a successful writer you have to have

thick skin.

There will be reviewers that will give you low ratings and readers that don't like your work. I recommend that you pay attention to the feedback, but take it in stride. My first book has received a few 3 star reviews. But that didn't stop me from promoting and selling my book, or writing more books. Some readers may not like even a well-written book because it's not their favorite genre or writing style that they are used to. You will never please all of the people all of the time. Take the feedback assess what is said and make adjustments if appropriate.

Make sure you know your craft.

As an author read books by other authors, attend writing classes and take feedback constructively. Don't simply dismiss the feedback because you disagree with it or because the majority of people disagree with the feedback. Seek the truth before dismissing it. Saying, "Well my friends like it, or other people say it's good" doesn't mean that your book is good. Your friends support you, which means they may not be willing to tell you the truth. Reality is your friends may not be writing professionals or in some cases avid readers either. If you really want to know what people who say your book is good truly think, ask a couple key questions, and give them permission to be honest. If you didn't know me, would you still buy this book? If the response is yes, with no explanation, that is probably an indication that your writing may need some tweaking. If people can't give you positive and negative feedback then you probably made a sale not a fan.

Your voice is unique, but there are some industry standards that you must adhere to like scene setting, character building, citing, and formatting. Those things can make the difference in selling 1,000 versus 10,000 books.

I know the growing trend is to release short stories or novellas as a series. Sometimes that is successful and sometimes it isn't. Don't be afraid to reach out to someone that is publishing a series and ask if they are willing to share their best practices with you. There are pros and cons to this publishing tactic; know what they are before going down that road.

Lastly, let's talk support.

Honestly, I could probably devote an attire chapter to support, but I will not get lost in the weeds on this one. Don't expect family, friends, co-workers, other authors or neighbors to support you. Yes, they should support you. Yes, it would be wonderful if they supported you and in some cases they will. But did you write your books for your family or the world?

People who know you have already decided whether or not they are going to buy your book. You should market to those who don't know you or your work. It works better for someone to buy your book and tell everyone who will listen about it. Than to have someone buy your book strictly to support you and they throw it in a drawer without ever reading it, much less sharing it with others.

Rather than expecting people to support you, encourage and engage their support. If you can peak their interest and they see value in your work, you don't have to ask for support. They will offer it. And value may be everything from an entertaining to informative read.

After reading this book you may have realized that your success as an author is based on 75 percent of your efforts and 25 percent about your book. Even a bad book marketed properly can become a best-seller.

Being an author and a smart businessperson equates to you working smarter, not harder. Find your creative niche and make it work for you. Don't worry if people will buy your book, or be concerned that there are other books on the same topic. A well- written book will sell. If something is of interest to you, I assure you that someone somewhere is interested in the subject too.

We have heard that more than once in our lives that we should plan and dream. However, the act of following through with the plan is the hardest thing for both business owners and authors to do. Don't be afraid to reach out to your audience, invite yourself to events, to network and be visible. Yes, in the beginning you will have to hunt for opportunities, but if you are authentic, consistent, and remain visible opportunities will chase you down.

Every missed opportunity to promote your work is self-defeating. Every attempt to promote yourself and your product keeps you in front of many prospective buyers, readers and listeners. Consider the book *Six Degrees of Separation,* and the theory it teaches: everyone in the world is connected to everyone else through a path of six people or fewer. With this in mind, why sabotage your success by not getting to that sixth person who may lead you closer to what you seek in life. The key is to develop a plan, decide how you choose to execute it and what you anticipate are the results to be gained.

I can imagine that you have reached the end of this book and may be disappointed that I have not specified what it takes to become a *bestselling* author. There is a method to my madness of why I purposely chose to omit the term *"bestselling"* from this book and use successful and well-known instead.

Here is why I chose not to discuss becoming a *bestseller*. Anyone that promises you that they can give you the secret formula to becoming a bestseller is not being 100% honest with you. If you ask 10 bestselling authors how they became a bestselling author, I can guarantee that you will receive 10 different answers. I didn't want to sell you a bill of goods that would leave you disenchanted.

Of course selling a million copies of your book will make you a bestseller. The challenge is actually getting those copies sold! Do not focus on making the bestsellers list, because you may be disappointed. Focus on giving readers value for their money, a read that they want to share with others, and watch how many books readers purchase.

Not all book retailers provide sales data to the various literary bestseller lists, which means depending on the location and other demographics you may or may not hit the New York Times bestseller list even though you've sold thousands of copies. But, on the flipside you can be an Amazon or Barnes & Noble bestseller. Also, it's possible to be a bestseller in a specific category and not make the overall bestselling list.

Shouting buy my book, buy my book, buy my book, will not grab or hold the attention of readers. As I said earlier, readers have to feel engaged and see the value in your book(s). Develop a strategy that will draw readers to you.

Becoming a bestselling author begins with having a passion for writing and/or the subjects that you write about, and it ends with building a fan base.

A solid fan base is truly what differentiates successful authors from writers that simply want to sell books. Anyone can sell a book, but not everyone can develop fans. Your fans will become advocates of your books and your brand. They will show up, buy your books and tell others about your books.

The truth is ***Write and Grow Rich*** contains all of the components necessary to be a bestselling author. The key is to find the component combination that works for you! There is no way that I could address every single scenario in this book, that is why I have developed courses that will assist you in putting the pieces together. Remember, I said this book is a road map, with the flexibility to find your way to your goal from wherever you are.

In order to ***Write and Grow Rich***, craft a book that is creative and engaging, develop a marketing strategy that targets the readers that you are trying to reach, and lastly be visible! If no one knows about you or your book, it is virtually impossible to sell it.

Remember: A Best Selling Author sells it best!

Next Steps

Next Steps

Next Steps

Next Steps

Questions

How do define success?

What are your goals for your book?

What are your goals as an author?

What do I expect from a publisher?

How do I plan to market my book?

Team Checklist

In order for you book to be a success, you have ensure that all bases are covered. As your budget allows, hire a dream team. A dream team is a group of people that you assemble based upon your needs and the goals that you have for your book. Here is a list of people that you may need.

❑ Editor

❑ Copy Editor

❑ Illustrator

❑ Graphic Designer

❑ Accountant

❑ Lawyer

❑ Assistant

❑ Web Designer

❑ Photographer

❑ Videographer

❑ Social Media Marketer

About the Author

As a dynamic speaker, celebrated author, Deondriea Cantrice has impacted many multifaceted audiences throughout the country with her life-changing message. She expertly entertains, educates, and inspires any audience with her tales of true life to keep them engaged and motivated.

Audiences connect with Deondriea through her vivacious, interactive style, and approachable manner. She incorporates into her presentations the skills she gained from many years of experience in the communications industry and being certified in Six Sigma Green Belt, customer service training, and stress and time management.

Deondriea is a highly sought after speaker because of her special talent for easily connecting with her audience, creating immediate feelings of trust and integrity. She is the author of several books, including Rhythm Can't Keep Time, Sometimes Love Just Ain't Enough; When Emotions Lie; You! Branding Yourself for Success; Tiptoes, Steel-Toes and Stilettos; and Write and Grow Rich. She has been named as a finalist for the Stiletto Woman in Business Award (SWIBA) for the 2014 Author of the Year and received the Distinction in Excellence Award from SWIBA.

Deondriea
CANTRICE
WWW.DEONDRIEA.COM
DEONDRIEA CANTRICE
DEONDRIEA CANTRICE
WHEN
Emotions
LIE
write and grow
RICH
TIP TOES
STEEL
TOES
AND
Stillettos
DEONDRIEA CANTRICE
DEONDRIEA CANTRICE
YOU!
BRANDING
YOURSELF FOR
SUCCESS!
Rhythm Can't Keep Time
Deondriea Cantrice
audible
an amazon company
iTunes
BARNES & NOBLE
BAM!
BOOKS-A-MILLION
amazon.com
@deondriea

Other books by Deondriea Cantrice

AFTER THE
Rain
A Guided Journal of
Discovering Passion and
Unleashing Purpose

Looking for a life coach? Hire Deondriea

f @deondriea

g+ @deondriea

Instagram @deondriea

in @deondriea

P @deondriea

You Tube @deondriea

NOTES

NOTES

NOTES

NOTES

NOTES

NOTES

NOTES

NOTES

NOTES

NOTES

NOTES

NOTES

NOTES

NOTES

NOTES

NOTES

NOTES

NOTES